CELEBRATING THE FAMILY NAME OF BOYD

Celebrating the Family Name of Boyd

Walter the Educator

SKB
Silent King Books
a WhichHead Entertainment Imprint

First Printing, 2024

Disclaimer

This book is a literary work; the story is not about specific persons, locations, situations, and/or circumstances unless mentioned in a historical context. Any resemblance to real persons, locations, situations, and/or circumstances is coincidental. This book is for entertainment and informational purposes only. The author and publisher offer this information without warranties expressed or implied. No matter the grounds, neither the author nor the publisher will be accountable for any losses, injuries, or other damages caused by the reader's use of this book. The use of this book acknowledges an understanding and acceptance of this disclaimer.

Celebrating the Family Name of Boyd is a memory book that belongs to the Celebrating Family Name Book Series by Walter the Educator. Collect them all and more books at WaltertheEducator.com

USE THE EXTRA SPACE TO DOCUMENT YOUR FAMILY MEMORIES THROUGHOUT THE YEARS

BOYD

Upon the highlands, wild and free,

Celebrating the Family Name of

Boyd

Where rivers carve through rock and tree,

A name is whispered, bold and proud

Boyd, a voice that sings out loud.

From rugged cliffs to fields untamed,

The Boyds have walked, their hearts aflame.

With grit and fire, they carved their way,

Through mist and dawn, through night and day.

A name that rises with the storm,

Unyielding, fierce, a steadfast form.

Like mountain air, sharp, clear, and bright,

The Boyds stand tall in morning's light.

In ancient lands where shadows roam,

The Boyds have made the earth their home.

Through every stone, through every tree,

Their roots are deep, their spirits free.

From warriors brave with swords in hand,

To builders shaping every land,

The Boyds have stood, unshaken still,

With iron hearts and iron will.

No tempest fierce, no roaring gale

Celebrating the Family Name of

Boyd

Could ever make a Boyd heart fail.

For in their veins there flows a pride

That mountains echo far and wide.

A family born of earth and sky,

With eyes that watch the eagle fly,

The Boyds have climbed where few would dare,

Their spirits wild, their souls laid bare.

In every battle they have fought,

In every dream they've fiercely sought,

The Boyds have never lost their way,

Their courage brightens darkest day.

Yet, in their strength, there’s warmth that lies,

Like summer sun in hazy skies.

A Boyd will fight, a Boyd will lead,

Celebrating the Family Name of

Boyd

But also know when hearts must heed.

Their homes are built with hands that care,

With love as strong as they can bear.

For in the Boyd, there's more than might—

There’s kindness deep, a softer light.

ABOUT THE CREATOR

Walter the Educator is one of the pseudonyms for Walter Anderson. Formally educated in Chemistry, Business, and Education, he is an educator, an author, a diverse entrepreneur, and he is the son of a disabled war veteran. "Walter the Educator" shares his time between educating and creating. He holds interests and owns several creative projects that entertain, enlighten, enhance, and educate, hoping to inspire and motivate you. Follow, find new works, and stay up to date with Walter the Educator™

at WaltertheEducator.com

www.ingramcontent.com/pod-product-compliance
Lightning Source LLC
LaVergne TN
LVHW010622070526
838199LV00063BA/5231
9798330480975